Miriam Moss was born in England, and has lived in the Middle East, Africa and China, and has travelled widely. She is an award-winning author whose books for Frances Lincoln include *This is the Oasis, This is the Reef* and *This is the Mountain,* all illustrated by Adrienne Kennaway. Miriam lives in Sussex with her family.

Adrienne Kennaway was born in New Zealand and studied at Ealing Art School in London and the Accademia de Belle Arte in Rome. She won the Kate Greenaway medal for *Crafty Chameleon.* Her previous books for Frances Lincoln include *Curious Clownfish* and *Rainbow Bird* by Eric Maddern. She lives in County Kerry, Ireland.

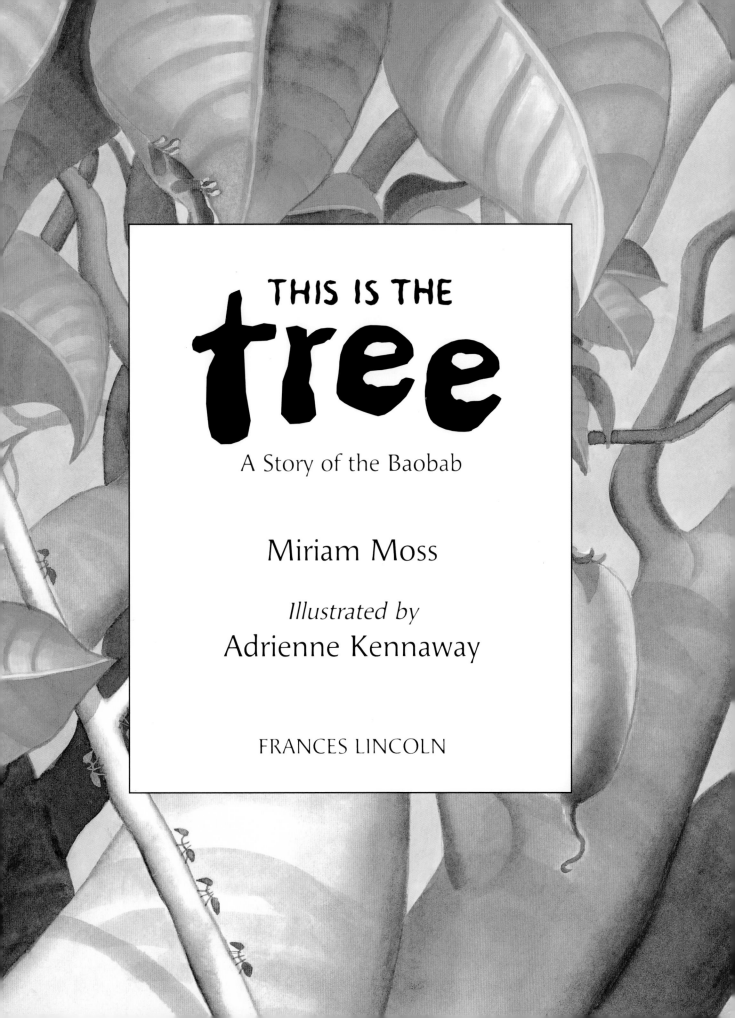

THIS IS THE
tree

A Story of the Baobab

Miriam Moss

Illustrated by
Adrienne Kennaway

FRANCES LINCOLN

This is the tree, when the world was still young,
that pushed up through the earth
as a small, tender shoot.

This is the tree, now old as a volcano,
standing alone
on the African plain.

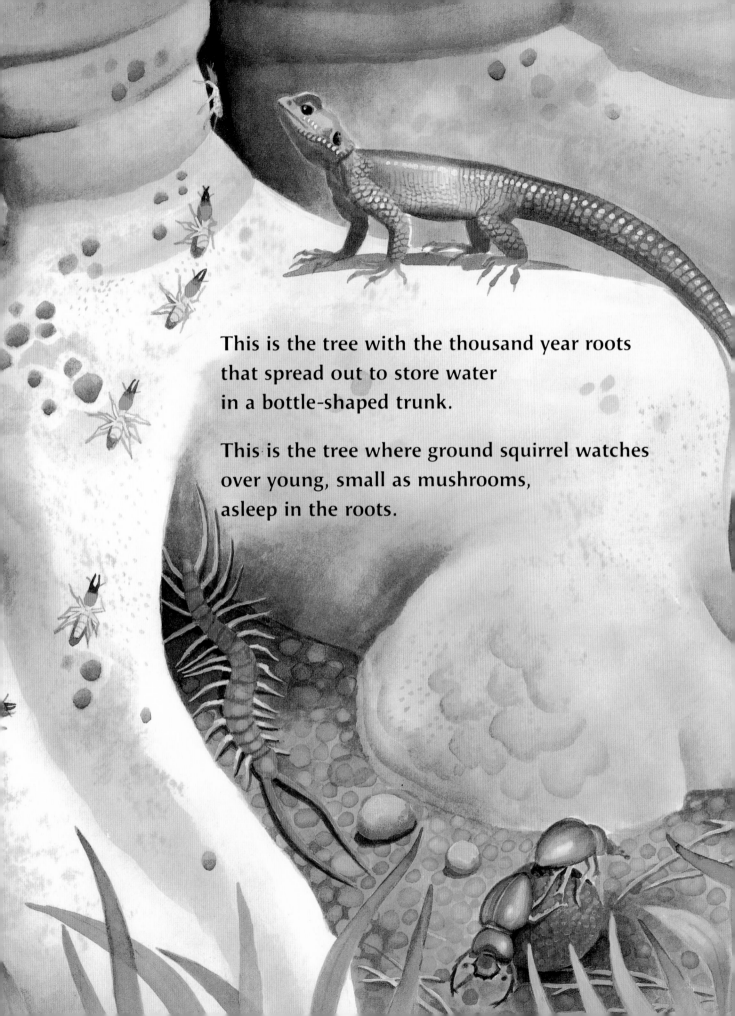

This is the tree with the thousand year roots
that spread out to store water
in a bottle-shaped trunk.

This is the tree where ground squirrel watches
over young, small as mushrooms,
asleep in the roots.

This is the tree with far-reaching branches
and cool shady places
for impala to dance in.

This is the tree where buffalo chooses
to sit sleepily chewing
in the heat of the day.

This is the tree that tosses and turns,
when high winds howl
and the sky turns black.

This is the tree dripping after the storm,
with dark-stained wrinkles
on knuckles and knees.

This is the tree with the huge rounded belly,
all lacy with shadows
in a sea of new grass.

This is the tree that the tribespeople visit
to cut bark, spilling insects
on red beaten earth.

This is the tree that is elephant's favourite,
that she scars with rough tusk-marks
to get to the core.

This is the tree a-dangle with fruit pods
that elephant crushes
to slurp up the pulp.

This is the tree along whose silver branches
chameleon treads slowly,
searching for flies.

This is the tree where turaco bird nests,
and where snake snoozes softly
with one beady eye.

This is the tree that bushbaby burgles,
plucking white, waxy petals
with fingers and toes.

This is the tree that dances with monkeys,
alive with their leapings
at the end of the day.

This is the tree where leopard lies darkly,
her eyes only glistening
as bats flitter by.

This is the tree in the silvery moonlight,
that points long crooked toes
to a sharp slice of moon.

This is the tree, old as a volcano,
the upside-down tree of the African plain.

This is
the Baobab Tree.

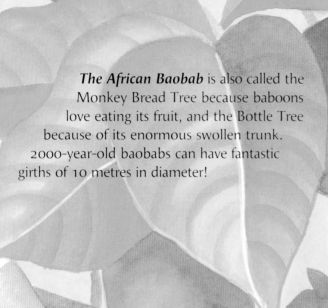

The African Baobab is also called the Monkey Bread Tree because baboons love eating its fruit, and the Bottle Tree because of its enormous swollen trunk. 2000-year-old baobabs can have fantastic girths of 10 metres in diameter!

Baobab leaves are not just eaten by cattle, browsing elephants and impala. They are rich in vitamin C and can be cooked like spinach or dried and made into soups and sauces. The leaves are also used as medicine to treat fevers, insect bites and diarrhoea.

Baobab flowers are large, white and waxy, with big yellow stamens. They begin to open around sunset but only last until the next morning. They give off a strong rotting smell which attracts bats, bluebottles and nocturnal moths.

Baobab fruits are woody hanging pods, covered in velvety yellow-brown hair. The seeds in ripe fruit are held in place by delicious sweet white pulp that tastes just like wine gums! When the heavy fruits fall from the tree, the woody casing cracks open and termites eat the fruit, leaving the seeds to be carried away by monkeys, baboons, squirrels and rats.

The hollowed-out trunks of baobabs are often used for storing water. A large tree can hold up to 2000 gallo Hollowed-out baobabs have been used for many weird and wonderful things. They have been prisons, stables bus shelters, dairies and a weaver's workshop. One baobab tree even had a flush toilet installed in it!

The baobab is home to many other insects and birds in addition to those mentioned in the book. King Baboon spiders, bees, mealy bugs, caterpillars and stick insects all live in the tree. Parrots, hornbills and kingfishers roost or nest in holes in the trunk, while lovebirds, barn owls and Wahlberg's eagles nest in the branches. And, dangling out on the ends of the highest branches, far away from predators, are the little buffalo-weaver birds' round basket nests.

Baobab roots can be cooked and eaten or made into red dye. They are also made into a dried powder to take as a medicine for malaria or as a mouthwash for toothache.

The strange shape of the baobab has inspired many stories. One says that the first baobab always complained wherever God planted it. In the end God became so fed up that he threw the tree away into the dry soil of the African plain – where it landed upside down! Some say that spirits live in the flowers, so that if you pick a flower, you will be killed by a lion. In Nigeria religious symbols have been found cut into the bark of ancient trees, suggesting that the trees were worshipped as fertility symbols in the past.

Baobab bark is extraordinary, because when it is cut or damaged it heals itself, just like our skin. Root bark is used to make strings for musical instruments or rope for making fishing nets. In parts of Africa, the fibres are woven into waterproof hats that are also used as drinking cups.

Baobab wood is very spongy as it is full of stored water. It is used to make plates, trays and floats for fishing.

In memory of Lucy Keeling, who edited this book with great skill and dedication, and who died, sadly, before it was completed. M.M. and A.K.

• ◆ •

For Tracy and the Harries Family, Thika, Kenya ~ M.M.

To my brother Patrick ~ A.K.

Frances Lincoln would like to thank James Morley and Sasha Barrow of the Royal Botanical Society Kew Gardens, and Joyce Pope, for their help.

First published in Great Britain in 2000 by
Frances Lincoln Children's Books, 4 Torriano Mews,
Torriano Avenue, London NW5 2RZ
www.franceslincoln.com

First paperback edition published in Great Britain in 2001

A catalogue record for this book is available from the British Library.

ISBN 978-0-71121-491-0

Printed in China

7 9 8

MORE TITLES IN THIS SERIES BY MIRIAM MOSS AND ADRIENNE KENNAWAY FROM FRANCES LINCOLN CHILDREN'S BOOKS

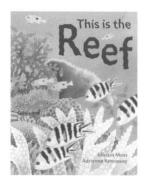

This is the Reef

Follow sharks, turtles and swirling shoals of fish in an extraordinary and inspiring journey through the Great Barrier Reef. This is a celebration of a unique and fragile eco-system and the marine life it feeds, shelters and protects. A perfect introduction to an ancient and breathtaking marine wilderness.

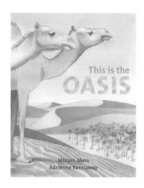

This is the Oasis

Have you ever wondered how anything survives in a hot desert climate? This is the celebration of an oasis – a green jewel in the Sahara – and its importance for the plant, animal and human life that surrounds it. Including facts about the Tuareg people, this is a perfect introduction to the harsh but beautiful desert wilderness and the life that it supports.

This is the Mountain

Mount Kilimanjaro in Africa is one of the great mountains of the world. This beautiful and inspiring book explores the vast richness of plant and animal life that it supports. Complete with further information pages about this extraordinary place and the threats to its unique habitats, this book is the perfect introduction to a precious environment.

Frances Lincoln titles are available from all good bookshops.
You can also buy books and find out more about your favourite titles,
authors and illustrators on our website: www.franceslincoln.com